Dublin, Cork & Galway Travel Guide

Attractions, Eating, Drinking, Shopping & Places To Stay

Christopher Reed

Copyright © 2014, Astute Press
All Rights Reserved.

No part of this publication may be reproduced, stored in a retrieval system, or transmitted, in any form or by any means without the prior written permission of the publisher, nor be otherwise circulated in any form of binding or cover other than that in which it is published and without similar condition being imposed on the subsequent purchaser.

If there are any errors or omissions in copyright acknowledgements the publisher will be pleased to insert the appropriate acknowledgement in any subsequent printing of this publication.

Although we have taken all reasonable care in researching this book we make no warranty about the accuracy or completeness of its content and disclaim all liability arising from its use

Table of Contents

Dublin 8
   Culture 9
   Location & Orientation 11
   Climate & When to Visit 12

Sightseeing Highlights 13
   Guinness Factory 13
   Temple Bar District 15
   Book of Kells at Trinity College 16
   Saint Stephen's Green 17
   Chester Beatty Library 18
   Saint Patrick's Cathedral 19
   Jameson Factory 20
   Dublin Castle 21
   Writers Museum 22
   National Museum of History & Archaeology 23
   National Gallery 24
   Christ Church Cathedral 25
   Kilmainham Gaol 26
   General Post Office 27
   Ha'Penny & O'Connell Bridges 28

Recommendations for the Budget Traveller 29
   Places to Stay 29
      Brook's Hotel 30
      Cassidy's Hotel 30
      Trinity Lodge 31
      Harding Hotel 32
      Abraham House 32
   Places to Eat & Drink 33
      O'Donoghue's 33
      Chez Max 34
      Temple Bar Pub 35
      Elephant & Castle 35
      Queen of Tarts 36
   Places to Shop 37
      Grafton Street 37

Henry Street & Mary Street 38
Temple Bar Shops 38
Stephen's Green Shopping Centre 39
George's Street Arcade 39

Cork 41
Culture 43
Location & Orientation 44
Climate & When to Visit 45

Sightseeing Highlights 48
Blarney Castle 48
Saint Fin Barre's Cathedral 49
Spike Island 51
Opera House 52
Fota Wildlife Park 53
Crawford Art Gallery 54
Mizen Head 55
Garnish Island & Tropical Gardens 57
Lisselan Estate & Henry Ford Ancestral Site 58
Blackwater Valley, Dinosaurs & Donkeys 59
Blackwater Valley 60
Donkey Sanctuary 60
Dinosaur Exhibition & Cafe 61
Fitzgerald's Park 62
Cork Public Museum 62
Lewis Glucksman Art Gallery 63

Recommendations for the Budget Traveller 66
Places to Stay 66
Paddy's Palace 66
Bru Bar Hostel 67
Stanley Guest House 67
Mountain View B&B 68
Annabella Lodge 69
Places to Eat & Drink 70
Farmgate Restaurant & Country Store 70
Cobh Heritage Centre Restaurant 71
O'Connors Seafood Restaurant 71
La Jolie Brise Pizza & Grill 72
Café Paradiso 73
Places to Shop 74
The English Market 74

Quills Woollen Market 75
Dunnes Stores 75
SuperValu 76
Homestore + More 77

Galway 78
Culture 81
Location & Orientation 83
Climate & When to Visit 84

Sightseeing Highlights 86
Galway Bay & Salthill Promenade 86
Turoe Pet Farm & Leisure Park 87
Inis Bó Finne (Island of the White Cow) 88
Leisureland Galway 90
Connemara National Park 90
Tropical Butterfly Centre 91
Aran Islands 92
Coole Park National Nature Reserve 92
Kylemore Abbey & Victorian Walled Gardens 94
Battle of Aughrim Interpretative Centre 95
Galway City Museum 96
Corrib Princess River Cruise 97
Galway Cathedral 98

Recommendations for the Budget Traveller 99
Places to Stay 99
Barnacles Hostel 99
Galway City Hostel 100
Lakeshore House 101
Árd Einne Guesthouse 102
Oak Lodge Portumna 103
Places to Eat & Drink 104
Breathnachs Bar 104
Pedro's Cafe & Grill 105
The Forge Pub & Eatery 105
The Bard's Den 106
Cupán Tae 107
Places to Shop 107
Penneys 107
Fallers Sweater Shop 108
Royal Tara 108
Ceardlann-Spiddal Craft & Design Studios 109

Thomas Dillon Claddagh Gold..110

Dublin

Ireland's capital city of Dublin is a thriving international centre of culture, music, food and nightlife. In Dublin you can drink Guinness at its source, bask in the splendour of ancient Cathedrals like Christ Church and Saint Patrick's, or enjoy the lively spirit of native Dubliners at a local pub in Temple Bar.

Dublin has a unique history, one that has been sculpted out of sorrow only to be transformed into something magical. It was named by the Vikings "Dubh Linn," meaning "Black Pool," and since these early times the city has seen more than it's share of dark days. Yet, at the end of it all Dublin has emerged triumphant, becoming one of the world's favorite destinations for relaxation and culture.

A trip to Dublin can be anything you wish it to be. As a rising global city, Dublin has all the offerings you can expect from a large city, while retaining its old world charm. On your visit you can view acclaimed international art at the National Gallery, stroll in a number of expertly designed gardens like St. Stephen's Green, or take a tour of a world-famous brewery. Dublin is a spectacular place for fun and excitement. The opportunities are endless, and your glass is always at least half full.

Culture

Irish culture is one of the most charismatic, vibrant cultures on earth; and the Irish are some of the most patriotic people, never afraid to say where they came from. In Dublin it's no different. They are passionate about their country, their music, their art and their history. They have created a lasting legacy because they have endured some of the most difficult and violent struggles. Yet, they have never lost their welcoming spirit. Anybody who's been to Dublin will tell you that once you sit down in a pub and drink a pint of Guinness with the locals, you'll become an honorary Irish citizen.

Dublin boasts an incredible artistic heritage as well, claiming some of the world's most famous writers and musicians. James Joyce, Oscar Wilde, Jonathan Swift, and dozens of other noteworthy names spent major parts of their lives in Dublin, and these great souls are commemorated in the Dublin Writer's Museum. Ireland's capital city is also home to the National Gallery and its impressive collection of Irish and European art.

One of the most famous aspects of Irish culture is undoubtedly its music. Contemporary musicians such as Sinead O'Connor and U2 claim Dublin as their home; but even with their global popularity, it is the traditional Irish songs and ballads that have captivated the heart of the world. There's nothing like an evening by the fireside in a Dublin pub, eating wholesome fare and drinking excellent beer with the natives, and listening to a local band play traditional music the way it has been performed for centuries.

In 2013, further evidencing the nation's spirit of friendship, Ireland is hosting a yearlong event known as the Gathering. This grand celebration was created as an invitation to those of Irish descent, and those who love Ireland, to come and immerse themselves in part of a twelve month festival of Irish culture and history.

Location & Orientation

Dublin can be found on the eastern coast of central Ireland, directly across from Galway and three hours northeast of Cork. It's across the Irish Sea from the British mainland, and 165 km south of Northern Ireland's capital Belfast. The territory of the city is 115 square kilometers with a population of 530,000.

The city is split in half by the River Liffey into the North and South sides. Multiple bridges line the waterway, the two most famous being the Ha'Penny and the O'Connell. The O'Connell Street Side is the North side, and the Grafton Street side is the South. In reading directions, a series of numbers are attached to locations in Dublin. All even postal codes can be found on the South Side, and all odd postal codes are on the North.

The greater metropolitan area of Dublin is home to many suburbs, and there are a few districts near the city centre which are of note. The most famous region of Dublin, Temple Bar, can be found slightly southwest of the O'Connell Bridge. Most of Dublin's main attractions can be found within 3 miles of this bridge, as it is officially declared to be the true centre of the city.

Climate & When to Visit

Because of its proximity to the sea, Dublin, Ireland has a maritime climate, one that sees moderate winters and bright, breezy summers. Average temperature in midsummer falls at around 20 degrees Celsius, and in winter it won't drop below 5 degrees Celsius. The most precipitation falls in autumn, in October, while the driest time is in February. Yet, always pack an umbrella as rain tends to fall most of the year without warning.

In recent years, Dublin has seen a surplus of tourism that has been unprecedented. This is especially true of the late summer months as most of Europe takes time for the holidays. July and August are the busiest times of the year in Dublin, and prices tend to reflect this fact. To beat the crowds there are two alternatives: either you can come in September, when the crowds have gone home and Dublin returns to a more manageable size, or in May, when the bustle is getting ready to begin.

Arguably, Dublin is its most beautiful in May and June, when the sun is shining radiantly, and the greenery becomes the lush, verdant shade for which the country of Ireland is famous; but no matter when you decide to visit Dublin, whether in the midst of winter or the highest point of spring, you will be welcomed, entertained, and dazzled by the charms of this magnificent destination.

Sightseeing Highlights

Guinness Factory

Guinness Storehouse, St James Gate, Dublin 8
+014538364
www.guinness-storehouse.com/

There are few pleasures in Dublin that are as famous as a freshly poured pint of Guinness, and no better place on earth to have it than in Dublin.

Ireland's capital city is the source of one of the finest beers known to man, and visitors to this grand place have the opportunity to see it being created from the ground up. The Guinness Factory is without doubt one of the most exciting attractions in Ireland, and a trip to Dublin wouldn't be complete without it.

Everything you could ever wish to know about the world famous black beer can be learned on a <u>Guinness Factory</u> tour. It opened its doors to the public for the first time in the late 1870s, but has been brewing the good stuff for more than 200 years. It is the country's <u>most exported product</u>, pumping out 1.8 billion pints internationally each year.

The factory is open year round, seven days per week, from 9:30 Am to 5:00 PM, and in July and August until 7:00 PM. Admission for adults is €15 and €11 for students. Visitors to the brewery receive a complementary pint of Guinness at the end of the tour at the storehouse's own Gravity Bar, offering a glorious panoramic view of the skyline of Dublin.

Temple Bar District

South Bank, River Liffey

One of the most iconic districts of Dublin is Temple Bar which possesses some of the city's best nightlife, restaurants, shopping, and recreation. Temple Bar is the city's cultural centre and a favorite place for locals and visitors to kick back over a pint while listening to fantastic music, or to walk down the streets linking arms in camaraderie on the way to the next pub.

Located on the South Bank of the River Liffey, Temple Bar spans from Fishamble Street to Westmoreland Street. The region is labeled after a wealthy gentleman, Sir William Temple, who used to own a home and gardens on the current property. The most noteworthy element about the area is, however, while the rest of Dublin's landscape was rapidly changing, becoming more industrialized, Temple Bar stayed the same. The cobblestone stone streets remained, the avenues kept their narrow structure, and the buildings themselves are as picturesque as ever.

In recent years, Temple Bar has received excessive "hype" as a result of its popularity with college students on holiday; but with Temple Bar enjoying yourself is a matter of timing. It's far too charming a place to pass up while in Dublin, and if you are afraid of the crowds, go during the day. Most of the bustle at Temple Bar happens in the evening, when the whole triangle becomes a party; but if a party is what you're looking for, then go in the evening, when the whole region is lit up in Irish jubilee.

Book of Kells at Trinity College

College Green,
Dublin 2 Ireland
+018961000
www.tcd.ie/

Trinity College is one of the most breathtaking architectural achievements of academia that Europe has to offer. It's Ireland's premier university and rivals some of the best schools in the world for quality and prestige. However, it's not the college itself that brings visitors in from around the world.

Many people have little interest in the structure of the buildings or the vibrancy of the classrooms at Trinity. Instead, they are focused entirely on one thing, something that has been a marvel in both the religious and literary worlds for hundreds of years: The Book of Kells.

The Book of Kells is housed on the campus's Old Library, a lengthy hall with lofty vaulted ceilings and 200,000 books. The work is one of the most extravagant of its kind, filled with incredible ornamentation and masterful calligraphy. Stripped of its fine furnishings, the book is a manuscript Gospel book in Latin, containing the four Gospels of the New Testament. It is the presentation of the text that makes it so exceptional. Celtic Monks in the ninth century AD painstakingly created in the Book of Kells a radiant piece of Insular artwork that has lasted for generations, filled with Celtic Knots, interlacing patterns, and intricate designs of human and animal life.

Admission to the Old Library to see the Book of Kells is €9. The work is ensconced in glass, and every few days the staff at the Old Library will turn the page. Also, keep in mind that for €9 you can see this section, but €1 more will include a tour of the whole campus. Tours are offered Monday through Saturday from 9:30 AM to 5:00 PM, and Sunday at varying times depending on season.

Saint Stephen's Green

St Stephens Green, Saint Stephen's Green,
Dublin, Co., Ireland
+014757816

Designed by master landscaper William Sheppard during the Victorian era, Saint Stephen's Green is a tranquil garden and park in the centre of Dublin town. The noise of the city can be overwhelming at times, and the park can be a needed refuge from the bustle of every day life. In the centre there is a large fountain, surrounded by a blanket of flowers in every color. There is an assortment of shady, grassy knolls, and often you can see men and women in business suits sprawled out on the ground at midday, during their lunch break.

It's a lovely place to stroll, to sunbathe, and to relax. Along the many circuitous pathways you can see statues of famous Irish historical figures, like Oscar Wilde for example, lounging on large rocks. The park is separated into nine different sections, called hectares, all brilliantly landscaped and conducive to tranquil recreation. Often there are free concerts in the park, especially in mid summer, so that guests can hear music while at their leisure.

You can find the park at the top of Grafton Street. The hours of operation are from 7:30 AM until sunset, but the venue is at its peak occupancy around noon, as it is a favorite spot for lunch picnics among locals.

Chester Beatty Library

Dublin Castle,
2 Dublin Ireland
+014070750
www.cbl.ie/

Holding a stunning collection of some of the world's greatest art, the Chester Beatty Library is one of Dublin's better organized and most interesting museums. It rivals some of the best galleries on the continent for its selection of ancient treasures, books, and art. The museum was founded in the 1950s by wealthy art collector Alfred Chester Beatty, who, in an act of philanthropic generosity, bequeathed his life's gatherings to the public.

Housed in Dublin Castle, the library offers a different perspective on the artistic contributions of various regions in the ancient world. Artifacts and pieces from China, Japan, and Persia are some of the highlights of this unique museum; but the galleries also contain objects from the transcultural religions of the ancient world. Most notably, in illuminate style similar to the Book of Kells, on exhibition at Chester Beatty are its ornate historical copies of the Qur'an.

If you are in any way fascinated by the history of the world, especially concerning art, culture, and religion, then a trip to Chester Beatty Library should be high on your list. Also, if it has any impact on your decision, admission to library is free. The doors are open from 10:00 AM to 5:00 PM most days of the week.

Saint Patrick's Cathedral

21-50 Patrick's Close
Off Clanbrassil St.,
Dublin 8, Ireland
+014754817
www.stpatrickscathedral.ie/

One of the jewels of architecture and design in the city of Dublin can be found at Saint Patrick's cathedral (officially: The Cathedral of the Blessed Virgin Mary and Saint Patrick).

Named for the country's patron saint, the site is said to be the earliest Christian holy place in all of Ireland. According to legend, it is here that Saint Patrick first baptized converts. Although many structures have existed on that sight over the last thousand years, the most current one dates from the Victorian era. It is the largest church in Dublin and the National Cathedral of Ireland.

The cathedral's Neo-gothic stylings leave the viewer in gaping awe at its majesty. The building is surrounded by lush gardens, allowing for rest and meditation for all who seek serenity. Church services occur daily within its sacred halls and are open to the public, but visitors are allowed to tour the interior of the cathedral for a small fee. Admission is €5.50 for adults and €4.50. Saint Patrick's Cathedral is also home to Ireland's Remembrance Day Ceremonies, observed since WWI in memorial to those who have lost their lives in the line of duty.

Jameson Factory

Bow Street
Smithfield, Dublin
+018072355
www.tours.jamesonwhiskey.com/

The national beer of Ireland is undoubtedly Guinness, but the national whisky is certainly Jameson.

Set on the grounds of the Old Jameson Distillery, a tour of Jameson's starting point is an interesting addition to any Dublin vacation. Many people find this tour to be better than its more famous Guinness counterpart because at Jameson a live guide leads you through the sights. These trained professionals tend to be engaging and even comedic at points as they explain the finer points of Irish whiskey to an eager audience.

It's no secret that to expertly make whiskey you'll need barley, water and yeast; but to transform this humble ingredients into something world famous is an art form that has been passed down through the generations in Dublin. On the tour, the entire process is recreated for the enjoyment of everyone, and at the end you are treated to a complementary glass of Ireland's greatest whiskey, or soda, if you prefer. Keep in mind that this tour is extremely popular, but it is possible to book reservations online in advance. Admission for adults is €13 and €7.70 for kids; and hours of opening are daily from 9:30 AM to 6:00 PM.

Dublin Castle

2 Palace Street, Dublin 2, Co., Dublin, Ireland
+016777129
www.dublincastle.ie/

A medieval stronghold, and one of the last remaining vestiges of medieval Dublin, Dublin Castle has been an iconic sight in the city centre since its construction in 1204.

Over the last several hundred years it has been used as a fortress, a prison, a courthouse, to its present use as royal banquet hall, governmental building, and museum grounds. The structure seen on the site today is not the original workmanship, and has seen almost continual renovation since the mid sixteenth century.

It's one of Dublin's most significant cultural assets, and tours are offered frequently. The site possesses museums, cafés, and gardens and has been host to many State Receptions and Presidential Inaugurations in recent years. Because of its function as an official governmental building, sometimes Dublin Castle is closed; but this is not often. Visitors are free to tour the grounds unguided, but if they wish for a guided tour, along with access to the inner rooms of the castle, admissions are €4.50 for adults and €2.00 for children. One of the highlights of the tour is the opportunity to go below ground, to see the hidden rooms beneath the castle that were used as jail cells for centuries.

Writers Museum

18 Parnell Square, Dublin, Ireland
+018722077
www.writersmuseum.com/

One of Dublin's most impressive, lasting legacies is its astounding literary tradition.

Ireland's capital city has been home to four Nobel Prize winners and noteworthy icons such as W.B. Yeats, Oscar Wilde, and James Joyce. Whether you are an avid reader or of moderate literary bent, one of the attractions best suited to an afternoon of historical consideration is the expertly organized Writers Museum. It has been open to the public since 1991 and is situated in a beautifully restored Georgian mansion five minutes away from O'Connell Street; in every nook and cranny of this grand house you'll find memorabilia from the lives and works of Dublin's greatest writers.

Jonathan Swift, George Bernard Shaw, and countless others are commemorated here in the Writers museum; but there's more to it than just the exhibitions. The museum hosts a lunchtime theater and readings and a number of conferences throughout the year. It's an ideal opportunity to immerse yourself in the brilliant works of these fine men and women. The museum is open daily from 10:00 AM to 5:00 PM, and admission is €7.50 for adults and €4.70 for children.

National Museum of History & Archaeology

Dublin, Ireland
+016777444
www.museum.ie/

Dublin's rising international status has not only played a large role in its popularity, but also in the overarching development of its unique culture.

One of the prime places in which to experience it's eclectic offering is at Ireland's National Museum of History and Archeology. The building that it is housed in, a Victorian inspired masterwork constructed by a duo of Cork architects, is considered to be a national historic landmark. The interior is filled with elegant balconies, intricate engravings, and magnificent art.

The galleries hosted within its walls are a tribute to the vibrant history of Ireland, hearkening to the triumph of the Bronze Age and marking important dates in time from then to now. Most remarkably, it contains a collection of medieval metalwork said to be the world's leading collection of Celtic metal artifacts. There are also a number of pieces from the Viking era. The hours of operation at the National Museum of History and Archeology are from Tuesday to Saturday from 10:00 AM to 5:00 PM, and on Sundays from 2:00 PM to 5:00 PM. Admission to all of Ireland's National Museums is free.

National Gallery

Collins Barracks, Benburb Street, Dublin 7, Co., Dublin, Ireland
+016777444
www.nationalgallery.ie/

One of the most expertly selected art galleries in Europe, containing some of the world's best Irish and European art, can be found in Dublin.

Situated in the popular Merrion Square, the National Gallery of Ireland is a worthy gallery by all accounts, and undoubtedly the premier collection in Ireland. A stroll through the building's corridors will bring you face to face with the works of Picasso, Rembrandt, Vermeer, and hundreds more.

It's one of the less discovered destinations of Dublin, as it is not directly in the centre of the city; and so, a visit to the National Gallery of Ireland will offer guests the chance to roam the nineteenth century halls in virtual solitude, guided by the sanctity of their thoughts, and by the inspiration of the art that surrounds them. The museum is open Monday through Saturday from 9:30 AM to 5:30 PM, and on Sundays from 12:00 PM to 5:30 PM.

Christ Church Cathedral

Christchurch Place
Dublin 8, Ireland
+016778099
www.christchurchdublin.ie

Dublin is a very unique city, with many incredible nuances that are often overlooked; for instance, it is home to not one, but two cathedrals, an unusual case for Europe. This Cathedral of the Holy Trinity was founded in the 11th century, and is one of the city's oldest buildings. It stands in striking contrast to the diversity of buildings that have sprung up around it, many of them containing modern stylings as a result of the economic boom of the 1990s in Dublin, while the appearance of the church remains ancient, almost stoic.

One of the most noteworthy aspects of Christ Church, and a fact that few people know about when visiting the cathedral, is that it contains an exceptional crypt. It is the largest in the British Isles, and contains a number of objects and relics in remembrance of a world long since past. There is a slight admissions fee of a few Euros for those who wish to tour the grounds without attending a service; but the services are open to the public, and are usually put on daily.

Kilmainham Gaol

Inchicore Road, Dublin,
Co., Dublin, Ireland
+014535984

One of the most famous events in the history of Ireland concerns the Easter Rising of 1916. Kilmainham Gaol was the holding place for the incendiary citizens who led these early revolts, and many of them were executed in the prison yard. Ultimately, like the Bastille is to Paris, Kilmainham is to the Irish. It is the symbol of their triumph as a people, a reminder of their independence; and today, it stands as one of the largest unoccupied jails in the world, on principle.

Kilmainham has been converted into a museum, and anybody who wishes can tour the exhibitions, and see firsthand the retelling of revolutionary Irish history. The exhibitions offer a realistic perspective of what life was really like on the interior, and verges on the macabre at many points. Admission to the museum is €6 for adults, and €2 for children and students. It is open from 9:30 AM to 6:00 PM Monday through Saturday, and from 10:00 AM to 2:00 PM on Sundays.

General Post Office

Lower O'Connell Street
Dublin
+017057064

The most iconic landmark for the Irish revolution can be found at the General Post Office on O'Connell Street. The building itself is massive, dominating the skyline as you wander down O'Connell; but more than its size, what's noteworthy about the Post Office is the role it played during the Easter Rising of 1916.

During this time, the original structure had served as the headquarters for the leaders of the uprising. In the violence, the building was damaged beyond repair. When the Irish Free State came into power many years later, they built a new Post Office in honor of their success. The only part of the old building that remains are the columns, which have become famous as they still contain the bullet holes of the 1916 events.

In spite of it's cultural significance, the General Post Office is an active postal carrier in Dublin, and you will see tourists alongside locals vying for space in the traditional interior, each there for completely different reasons.

Ha'Penny & O'Connell Bridges

Over the River Liffey

The shimmering waters of the River Liffey have been implanted in the hearts of Dubliners for as long as there has been a Dublin, and the bridges that cross them are worthy sights to visit while in the capital city of Ireland. They are architectural masterworks in their own right, each with a unique history.

The O'Connell Bridge, the younger of the two, was opened in 1882, and named for Dublin icon Daniel O'Connell, one of the first activists for Catholic emancipation in Ireland. The bridge is the only bridge in Europe that's as wide as it is long.

The Ha'Penny Bridge was Dublin's only pedestrian bridge across the River Liffey until 2000. When it opened in 1816, a toll was instituted to any who would cross it, a half penny. The toll stuck for more than a hundred years, and the name for now almost twice that. The unique structure of the bridge is one of the most emblematic in Dublin, as much a part of the city as the Spire, the General Post Office, and the Dubliners themselves.

Recommendations for the Budget Traveller

Places to Stay

Picturesque Georgian architecture on secluded cobblestone streets, bustling hostels in the heart of the city, and cozy Bed and Breakfasts, Dublin offers its guests a variety of accommodations that fit every style and taste. Many hotels provide comfortable lodgings and complementary British breakfasts, complete with all the tasty drippings. Prices in the city centre are usually affordable, but no matter what your budget, there's a perfect place to stay for you in Dublin.

Brook's Hotel

59-63 Drury Street, Dublin City Centre
Dublin, Co., Dublin, Ireland
+016704000
www.brookshotel.ie/
€75-€150

Located within walking distance of Dublin's centre and Grafton Street Shopping, Brook's hotel is a classic, comfortable hotel with all the necessary amenities. The building itself is cozy, with 98 rooms expertly decorated. There are several restaurants located on site for your convenience, along with free wi-fi, and cable. Make sure you ask for a room away from the road if you want to ensure a quiet night.

Cassidy's Hotel

Cavenish Row off O'Connell Street,
Dublin 1, Co., Dublin, Ireland
+018780555
www.cassidyshotel.com/
€50-€100

This historic hotel is great for the budget traveler.

Located on a cozy side road off of the bustling O'Connell Street, Cassidy's Hotel offers a comfortable stay and quiet atmosphere. The rooms are spacious and inviting, and the breakfast buffet is worth waking up for. Each of the 114 rooms is soundproofed, providing the opportunity for peaceful sleep to each of its guests.

Trinity Lodge

12 Frederick Street South Dublin 2,
Co., Dublin, Ireland
+016170900
www.trinitylodge.com/
€75-€100

This unique hotel couldn't be in a better location. The four-star accommodation known as Trinity Lodge is near to the famous landmark Trinity college, and is within walking distance of some of the best highlights of the city. It's a smaller hotel, with only 23 rooms, but this only adds to its charm. The hotel is sophisticated and elegant, occupying the floors of three beautifully restored Georgian townhouses. Trinity Lodge is the epitome of comfort and class.

Harding Hotel

Copper Alley, Fishamble Street
Dublin, Co., Dublin, Ireland
+016796500
www.hardinghotel.ie/
€50-€100

In a bustling metropolitan city, the important thing is not always the quality of where you stay, but how close it is to everything. At Harding Hotel, you have the best of both worlds. The hotel is literally right in front of Christ Church Cathedral, and a stone's throw from Jameson's Distillery. The rooms are clean, and the staff is <u>exemplary</u>. It's undoubtedly one of the best places to stay during your visit to Dublin.

Abraham House

83 Gardiner Street Lower
Dublin 1, Co., Dublin, Ireland
+018550600
www.abraham-house.ie/
€15-€40

Convenient, clean, and right in the heart of everything, Abraham House is a hostel that separates you from the noise of the city street, but puts you close to the important sights.

Its rooms are modest, but full of modern amenities, and breakfast is free. It's less than five minutes from O'Connell Street, and the friendly staff are more than willing to help with directions or to recommend a great restaurant. Also, if you have an early flight, the airport bus stop is right across the street.

Places to Eat & Drink

There's nothing in Ireland that's quite like a pub, and some of the best in the country are in Dublin. There's nowhere else that the Guinness is this fresh, the people are this friendly, or the atmosphere is as lively. Nowadays, however, pubs aren't the only options. Gastronomy is a rising field in the capital city of Ireland, and renowned chefs from all over the world have flocked to these parts to open up restaurants. With such incredible diversity, you can't go wrong when looking for a great meal in Dublin.

O'Donoghue's

15 Merrion Row, Dublin 2, Dublin, Ireland
+016607194
http://www.odonoghues.ie
€12-€25

There are hundreds of pubs in Dublin, but few that emit the charm and character that can be had at O'Donoghue's.

The most important asset that a Dublin bar should have is the ability to pour a perfect pint of Guinness, and at O'Donoghue's you can be assured that it will be perfect every time. The place is crowded, but that's part of the overall experience; however, if you want to be sure to find a table, make sure you get there by 7:00 PM. If you arrive early you can also take advantage of the early bird specials.

Chez Max

1 Palace St., Dublin
Dublin 2, Ireland
+353016337215
http://www.chezmax.ie
€20-€45

Chez Max is certainly among the best places to eat in Dublin. The cuisine is French, and the restaurant serves authentic fare that's of superb quality. Guests can choose from a list of aromatic wines, nibble on goat cheese wrapped in phyllo dough, and feast on mussels à la basque. The ambiance is simplistic and romantic and the waiters are friendly. A meal at Chez Max is truly one of the best you'll find in Dublin.

Temple Bar Pub

47/48 Temple Bar
Dublin 2, Dublin, Ireland
+016725286
http://www.thetemplebarpub.com/
€12-€25

To visit Dublin and not drink a pint of the good stuff at the Temple Bar Pub would be akin to not visiting Dublin at all.

This iconic nighttime destination has become synonymous with the Dublin experience, consistently providing a unique atmosphere complete with noisy people, traditional Irish music, and great beer. However, this place becomes extremely crowded during certain points of the week (and year), so unless you want to fight your way through the door, perhaps try it out during lunchtime.

Elephant & Castle

18 Temple Bar, Dublin 2, Dublin Ireland
+016793121
http://www.elephantandcastle.ie/
€12-€25

Chicken wings aren't always perceived to be a staple of the Irish diet, yet, they are the specialty of one of Dublin's most noteworthy restaurants.

The Elephant and Castle is a quirky eating establishment that serves up classic bar food with a twist. The menu is very simple, with only a few options, but the service is exemplary. It's one of the few places in Temple Bar where beer isn't the most important item offered, and as a result the Elephant and Castle has become a haven for the sober and hungry. When at Elephant and Castle, and given the choice between the burger or the wings, choose the wings, you won't regret it.

Queen of Tarts

Dame Street
Cork Hill
Dublin 2, Dublin, Ireland
http://www.queenoftarts.ie/
€8-€20

Dublin is no longer the hub of libertine behavior that it used to be, in recent years it has developed into a sophisticated global city. This transformation is evidenced by a wealth of elegant culinary options, one of them being the decadent Queen of Tarts. This delightful modern patisserie is one of the best spots in Ireland for breakfast or afternoon tea. Their menu is diverse, and their baked goods are too tempting to pass up. Don't stay at the hotel when it's time for breakfast, indulge your senses with tea and cake at Queen of Tarts.

Places to Shop

Dublin is not only a fashionable city, but it's also a walkable city. As a result, it's full of crisscrossing patterns of lengthy arcades and pedestrianized shopping districts. The regions of shopping, like everything else in Dublin, are separated into two districts. On the North side you will find bargains, oddities, and independent boutiques; and on the South side you will discover endless avenues of designer labels and international brands. However, if you're in the mood for something whimsical, there's certainly no shortage of zany Irish themed accoutrements in the many souvenir shops.

Grafton Street

South River Bank
Dublin, Ireland

Grafton Street is an international gathering place for people from all regions of the world. Anything you could wish to find can be found on this metropolitan street. If you want shoes, there's Korky's, Barrets, or the more recognizable Nine West. It's also home to a range of department stores selling everything from clothes, to electronics. Also, nestled between designer wear and independent boutiques are the ubiquitous souvenir stores, where eclectic "relics" of Irish culture can be bought for a few Euros.

Henry Street & Mary Street

North River Bank
Dublin, Ireland

The Streets of Henry and Mary weave together to form one of Dublin's best shopping districts. All along the avenue are historic Georgian buildings, and many of the shops held within them are full of Irish charm. Here you'll find designer stores as well, but the feel of the district is less formal than its counterpart in Grafton. More local Dubliners are found here, going about their daily business. As a result, you'll have more luck finding bargains in these parts, as the prices are less likely to be hiked up in honor of tourists.

Temple Bar Shops

2 - 5 Wellington Quay
Temple Bar, Dublin 2, Ireland
+35317030700
http://www.visit-templebar.com/

Temple Bar is without doubt one of the most famous districts in all of Dublin, and the shopping matches its reputation. This is the spot for more trendy styles, targeting a younger, thriftier audience. Rows upon rows of secondhand stores line the narrow streets of the Temple Bar triangle. Here you can find everything from jewelry, to novelty and memorabilia, to fashion boutiques, and usually at decent prices.

Stephen's Green Shopping Centre

Top of Grafton Street
Dublin, Ireland
www.stephensgreen.com/

Stephen's Green Shopping Centre is as much an architectural wonder as it is a modern shopping plaza. Located at the top of Grafton Street, at the mouth of Stephen's Green. The centre is on two levels and has more than 100 stores, many of them internationally recognized brands. If you're looking for something at Stephen's Green Shopping Centre that's not run of the mill, check out The Banana Tree. It's a novelty shop, and you're sure to find something interesting.

George's Street Arcade

South Great George's Street
Dublin, Co., Dublin, Ireland
+012836077
www.georgesstreetarcade.ie/

This charming hub for unique trinkets is one of the city's hidden jewels. There are thousands of novelty souvenir stores in the city, but only at George's Street Arcade can you be sure that what you discover is one of a kind.

It's an indoor market, reminiscent of the Victorian age, lined with endless rows of interesting shops. Here you can find anything from antiques, to jewelry, to local art. Even if you aren't planning to buy anything, a stroll through George's Street Arcade is an experience that's worth your while.

Cork

Cork is Ireland's southern-most and largest county. Its lovely villages are surrounded by verdant green hills and its lowlands rise to the Shehy Mountains on the Kerry border. Cork's varied coastline has rocky inlets which merge with the tiny villages that are squeezed between the beaches and green fields.

Tiny islands dot the coast of Cork with Carbery's Hundred Isles to the west being especially beautiful. Some islands are deserted with just wildlife, others have just a few residents and some are privately owned.

It is possible to visit some of the islands by ferry or on foot at low tide. The coastline draws people to see the many sharks and whales that can be seen from there. Minke whales, fin whales, pilot whales and basking sharks are all frequent visitors.

The food in County Cork is of the highest quality and much of it is organically produced. There is plenty of locally reared lamb, pork and beef with homegrown vegetables. The lush green grass is ideal grazing for the cows that produce creamy milk that is turned into delicious farmhouse cheeses. There are specialist food shops and farmers markets all over the county and many of the restaurants serve the freshest of produce.

In the north of the country the Blackwater River Valley is great for fishing, riding and historic architecture. For golf lovers, the County Cork has around 30 golf courses, many of them rich in history and with challenging and exceptional golfing terrain.

Cork City is the largest town in County Cork and also the capital. The city centre is built on an island created by the two channels of the River Lee that separate at the western end only to join again in the east. There are various docks and quays leading to Cork Harbour and Lough Mahon, the natural harbour in Cork is one of the largest in the world. The city is vibrant and bustling with communities from Lithuania, Hungary and Poland which gives a multi-cultural feel to its many festivals, bars, restaurants and live music events.

Originally a settlement for monks and founded in 606 AD by St. Fin Barre, Cork is the third largest city in Ireland after Dublin and Belfast. The city is headquarters to several world famous companies and the pretty Georgian and Victorian parts of the town are being changed by the renewal of the inner city areas and by growth.

Culture

Corkonians refer to themselves as The Rebels and see themselves as different from the rest of Ireland. The county is often called the Rebel County and its citizens are often seen wearing items that celebrate The People's Republic of Cork. There is a lot of rivalry between Dublin and Cork. Cork's accent is different to the rest of the island, with a lot of the words being in a more high-pitched tone than would normally be associated with an Irish accent.

There are many art centres in Cork city and throughout the year numerous festivals take place. In 2005 Cork was designated European City of Culture. The city's festivals take place on Grand Parade and St. Patrick's Street and there are food stalls in the streets serving traditional Cork foods like tripe, crubeens and drisheen.

The Irish people are great football and rugby fans and Munster is presently one of European Rugby's best teams. Their home ground is at Musgrave Park so try to catch a game while you are in Cork. For football lovers Turner's Cross Stadium is just outside the city where home matches are held in season. You can watch a hurling game at Páirc Uí Caoimh, the home of Cork GAA (Gaelic Athletic Association for the Preservation and Cultivation of National Pastimes).

For lovers of Guinness and beer, on a Friday night at 8pm go to the post office (GPO) on Oliver Plunkett Street for the Cork City Pub Crawl. A group of local guides take tourists and residents alike to some of the fun pubs in the city. There is a charge of €10 and includes shots on the way and after entry into a pub. If you are up for the "craic" (chat) why not attend?

Location & Orientation

County Cork is the southernmost county in Ireland. It is located in the south west of the country and covers an area of 2,879 square miles (7,457 km^2). The population is 518,000 and it is second only to Antrim county in size. The scenery is stunning and varies from flat deserted beaches backed by soaring cliffs to green pastures inland and mountainous regions in the distance. Around 10 % of the land is covered in peat and just over 11% is woodlands and forests. This area of Ireland is known for its peninsulas and Brow Head is the southernmost point.

The transport links to the rest of Ireland are good with international connections from Cork airport going to many popular destinations in Europe. The airport is just outside of Cork and is well connected by bus and taxi to the city centre. The roads have been vastly improved over the years particularly in and around the city centre. The M8 motorway links the 136 miles (220 km) between Cork and Dublin making travelling between the two cities quick and easy. The city council are very pro-active in trying to reduce the carbon footprint and a car sharing scheme is actively promoted. The city is also very bicycle friendly with many cycle paths and bike stands.

The main rail line into Cork is from Dublin with hourly departures. There also trains to Tralee, Killarney, Limerick and Galway. Connections round the city of Cork are provided by the Cork Suburban Rail system. (There are plans to build a light rail system in the city but due to the recession this project has been put on hold until 2017).

Climate & When to Visit

Ireland has a changeable but mild climate with plenty of rainfall but no real extremes of weather. There can be about 11 days of snow but it very rarely stays on the ground for more than a couple of days. This is usually only at the airport as it is quite a bit higher than Cork city itself, where little snow ever falls.

The southwest coast of County Cork is particularly pleasant and frost-free all year round. The Gulf Stream brings in warm air that keeps the temperature slightly higher than elsewhere in Ireland. This encourages the growth of sub-tropical vegetation along the coast with beautiful azaleas and rhododendrons bringing colour to the area from April to May. Cork city has just under four hours of sunshine a day on average with only about nine weeks of the year receiving no recordable sunshine.

The temperature ranges from 3° to 7 °C (37° to 45° F) in the winter months to from 12° to 19° C (54° to 66° F) in the summer. For about half of the year rain falls at some point through the day so an umbrella is useful to carry. Cork city is also prone to fog, mostly in the mornings and through the winter months.

For a holiday any time of the year in the county of Cork it is best to take clothes for all weathers. For hiking and walking holiday's stout, sensible shoes or boots are a must for a good grip on slippery slopes. Layers of clothing are always best any time of the year as mornings and evenings can be chilly but through the middle of the day it can be warmer. There is probably no need for really thick coats, gloves and hats in the winter like in some countries but a decent coat will be necessary, preferably rainproof.

Sightseeing Highlights

Blarney Castle

Blarney
Co. Cork
Tel: +353 21 438 5252
http://www.blarneycastle.ie/

Kissing the Blarney Stone is an activity that most everyone has heard of. 400,000 people a year make the journey to Blarney Castle and do just that. It is no easy feat to kiss the legendary stone. After climbing a spiral staircase to the upper reaches of the square tower and making your way round the walkway at the top a little bit of agility is needed before your lips meet the cold stone. For hundreds of years the only way to kiss the stone was by being dangled over the edge by your legs! However, safety now prevails and an iron railing gives support so you can lean backwards for the all important mouth-on-stone experience.

The world blarney best describes the way the Irish speak. The Irish are reputed to have the gift of the gab, mixed with flattery and wit. Hopefully once you have performed minor acrobatics to kiss the Blarney Stone you will never be lost for words which is why it is sometimes referred to as the Stone of Eloquence.

The castle was built around 600 years ago by Cormac MacCarthy, one of the greatest chieftains of Ireland, with the stone being set into the tower in 1446. There is much more to Blarney castle than just the stone, Rock Close is a magical place where druids once lived and the Wishing Steps and Witches Kitchen all have a timeless appeal of their own. The Poison Garden is home to some deadly plants while other gardens are filled with ferns, and in the springtime thousands of bulbs erupt into a sea of colour.

You can visit Blarney Castle every day of the year. The castle is open from 9am every day, closing around 6.30pm depending on the time of year or at sundown in the winter months. Admission prices are €12 per adult, €10 for students and OAP's and €5 for children. There is a family pass at €30 for two adults and two children.

Saint Fin Barre's Cathedral

Cathedral Office
Library House
Dean Street
Cork
Tel: + 353 21 496 3387
http://cathedral.cork.anglican.org/

Saint Fin Barre's Cathedral is a fine Gothic building from the 19th century.

The front is impressive and viewed from the back there is a beautiful golden angel blowing her trumpet perched high on the tower. The site the cathedral stands on has been in use since 606 AD when Saint Fin Barre founded a monastic school in Cork. Since then Christian learning and worship have always taken place here. Saint Fin Barre is believed to be buried in the graveyard of the cathedral near to the east end.

The cathedral was designed by William Burges in 1862. He won a design competition and the total building costs were £100,000. The majority of the materials to build the cathedral came from local sources with red Cork marble lining the walls and Cork limestone being used for the exterior structure. The inside is made from Bath stone with splendid stained glass windows and a beautifully decorated chancel.

The cathedral is only a short walk from the centre of Cork. The opening hours are Monday to Saturday 9.30am to 5.30pm all year round and Sunday 12.30 to 5pm in April and November. A small fee is charged of €5 per adult and €3 per child. There is a gift shop selling items from around the local area as well as cathedral related gifts and all profits are used to maintain the cathedral. An unusual gift from the cathedral is to sponsor a pipe in the Cathedral Organ which costs €20-€500 depending on the size of the pipe.

Spike Island

Cork Harbour
http://www.spikeislandcork.ie/

This 103 acre island in Cork Harbour was originally used by 7th century monks as their home but over the years it has been used for defence and also as a prison. The fort that dominates is the island is now being developed as a tourist attraction. Right up until the end of the 20th century the island was still used as a correctional facility for youths and in 1985 the criminals rioted and took the prison officers hostage. One of the accommodation buildings caught fire during the riots and is now known as the Burnt Block. The facility finally closed in 2004.

Tours can be taken across to the island from Cobh in the summer months and visitors can see the gun emplacements, prison cells and the fort. There is a café in the prison which does have a more varied menu than the staple prison diet of bread and water or you can take a picnic and enjoy a day exploring the island. There is a lot of development going on to make the island visitor friendly but that doesn't detract from the splendour of the scenery or the history hiding in the walls of the fort.

There are two ferry departure points for Spike Island, Monkstown and Cobh. Times vary so it is better to check on-line. Admission to the island and fort is free but there is a charge for the ferry, €8 per adult, €5 per child or a family ticket for two adults and two children or one adult and three children for €20.

Opera House

Emmet Place
Cork
Tel: + 353 21 427 0022
www.corkoperahouse.ie

Cork Opera House is the premier venue in southern Ireland for not just opera but dramas, concerts and dance. Despite a rather chequered history of fire and being dismantled brick by brick and moved to Emmet Place the Opera House survives to serve a new generation of opera and music lovers. This 160 year old institution in the heart of Cork City has gone through many upgrades to the seating, catering facilities and acoustics and there are two public bars as well as corporate boxes, a café and shop. The auditorium can hold 1,000 people and 70 musicians can be accommodated in the orchestra pit.

Shows range from performances for small children to ladies only naughty nights, classical music to disco fever. International and local stars perform in shows to entertain all the family with musicals from through the years and pantomimes at Christmas. Whatever your taste there is bound to something on to suit you.

Opening times and ticket prices vary according to the show you wish to see. All the information is on the website or bookings can be made by calling the box office or through ticket agencies. The box office is open Monday to Saturday 10am to 5.30pm on non-show days and 10am to 7pm on show days. Sunday 10am to 7pm show days only.

Fota Wildlife Park

Carrigtwohill
County Cork
Tel: +353 21 481 2678
www.fotawildlife.ie/

Fota Wildlife Park opened its gates in 1983 and has been improved and developed ever since then to provide housing for thousands of animals and birds. The main object of the park is to provide an excellent standard of care and conservation for all its inhabitants. The 75 acre park on Fota Island is home to 50 species of birds and 30 species of mammals. Some of the smaller ones like squirrels and lemurs roam freely among the visitors, while the larger species like giraffes and bison are behind see-through protective barriers.

Cheetahs love to work for their dinner, so the keepers have devised a way of doing this and amusing the audience at the same time. Children love to watch as the food is suspended above the cheetahs on a wire at about 10 feet off the ground. This is on a moving cable so the cheetahs have to chase the food at about 65 mph before they can eat their dinner. Not far away kangaroos hop about on the lush green grass while nearby penguins and seals splash about in the ocean pools.

The development of Fota was done with visitors of all ages in mind and to maximise income. The park is a self-financing organisation as well as a registered charity and relies on takings to survive. There are many conservation courses and children's workshops to take part in and corporate packages are available as well.

On site facilities include the Oasis and Savannah Cafés, one at each end of the park where hot and cold meals can be purchased. The Serengeti Gift Store has some great reminders of your day at Fota as well as having a selection of drinks and snacks. There are plenty of children's play areas for when the little ones, or you, need a break from admiring the animals.

Fota Wildlife Park is open Monday to Saturday at 10am and on Sundays at 10.30am. Closing time is 6pm all week. Adults pay €14.00, children, students, OAP's and disabled pay €9 and toddlers under three are free. There are several combinations of family tickets available so have a look online to see if you can save before you go.

Crawford Art Gallery

Emmet Place
Cork
Tel: +353 21 480 5042
www.crawfordartgallery.ie

Over 200,000 visitors flock every year to see the displays of contemporary and historic art at the Crawford Art Gallery. The building that now houses the gallery started life in 1724 as Cork's Custom House and many extensions have been made over the years. Located in the centre of Cork city the gallery has also been a design school and part of the South Kensington School system.

There is a fine collection of Roman and Greek statues. The statues were cast by Antonio Canova who had been commissioned by Pope Pius VII to copy the ones in the Vatican. The rest of the collection has grown steadily and in 1990 there were some 1500 pieces which were later listed in an illustrated catalogue in 1992. Since then many more works have been added and the total of paintings, sculptures, prints and other works of art is over 2,500.

As well as the static collections there are temporary exhibitions and outreach programmes so that the art work can be shared. The gallery is open Monday to Saturday from 10am to 5pm and admission is free. There is a café where lunches are available and on Thursdays only an evening menu is offered.

Mizen Head

The Harbour Road
Goleen,
County Cork
Tel: +353 28 35115
www.mizenhead.ie/

Mizen Head is an exhilarating place to visit, where two currents meet and the waves coming from the Atlantic Ocean crash onto the rocks. The most south-westerly point of Ireland was chosen for a lighthouse in 1906 to try to stop the huge loss of life and ships on the treacherous rocks. Three lighthouse keepers manned the light day in and day out until 1993 when an automated process was put in place.

The locals were reluctant to see the lighthouse and surrounding area be abandoned after so many years of service so they took matters into their own hands and created the Mizen Tourism Co-operative Society Ltd. The Mizen Vision visitors centre includes a tour of the peninsula and plenty of things to see in the centre itself. The Fastnet Rescue Tide Clock, SS Irada Propellor and the Geology of the Mizen are just a few of the exciting things to see in this wild and wonderful location.

The visitor's centre has a large car park and that is the end of the road for vehicles. To see the actual lighthouse there is a 550 yard (495 metre) walk along the cliffs and over the footbridge before you get there. There are 99 steps on the way down and the walk across the Arched Bridge is quite spectacular, suspended high over the waters of the Atlantic. The scenery as you walk down the path is pretty amazing and it is easy to imagine ships being flung onto the jagged and dangerous rocks while the sailors were thrown helplessly round the decks. The walk down to the lighthouse and tour of the inside takes about one to one and a half hours.

There is plenty to do and see and it would be an ideal place for a picnic and for some brisk walks in the salty sea air. If you don't fancy soggy sandwiches there is a café run by the local people that serves good home-cooked food and a selection of drinks and snacks. The Gift Shop@the Mizen is a lovely little shop filled with all things maritime as well as postcards and maps.

Visits to the Gift Shop and Mizen café are free but there is a small charge to carry on down to the lighthouse. Opening hours are 10am to 6pm June to August and 11am to 4pm November to mid-March. An adult ticket is €6, OAP/student €4.50 and children under 12 pay €3.50. There is a family ticket for €18 for two adults and up to three children.

Garnish Island & Tropical Gardens

Glengarriff,
County Cork
Tel: +353 27 63040
www.garnishisland.com/

Take the 15 minute ferry ride across to Garnish Island and wander through the beautiful gardens. A combination of micro-climate, sheltered woodlands and Gulf Stream means that many exotic and rare species flourish here. The woodlands were planted 100 years ago and include a Martello Tower from 1805, a Grecian Temple and an Italian Garden and Tea House.

The ferries leave Glengarriff harbour every 30 minutes and and the way to and from the islands you can see the seal colony. Around 250 seals swim round and bask on the rocks posing for photos. They are so used to the ferries that they just take no notice whatsoever. Disabled visitors can use the ferries although not all of Garnish Island is accessible to wheelchair users. There is a small restaurant on the island for light lunches and refreshments.

Departure times are between 10am and 4pm Monday to Saturday and 1pm to 5pm on Sundays. The entry fee for Garnish Island is €4 per adult, €3 OAP and €2 per child. There is a separate charge for the ferry crossing.

Lisselan Estate & Henry Ford Ancestral Site

Lisselane
Clonakilty
County Cork
Tel: +353 23 883 3249
www.lisselan.com/

The French Chateau style house on the Lisselan Estate was built between 1851 and 1853 and in the late 1800's more rooms and extensions were added. Visitors are drawn to this beautiful house in its riverside setting to walk through the magnificent gardens and see the exhibition of Vintage Ford Vehicles. The Henry Ford Ancestral Museum is on the estate and there are several vehicles for visitors to see. Although Henry Ford was born in America his father and grandfather were both born in Ireland. His grandfather, John Ford, farmed 30 acres of land on the Lisselan Estate.

The gardens are planned so that the changes through the seasons can be seen by everyone and enjoyed to the full. In spring the daffodils and camellias bloom into riotous colour and by May the bluebells make a stunning carpet along the long avenue.

In summer the herbaceous border takes pride of place and through August and September through to winter the stunning colours of the many varieties of fuchsias display their two-toned flowers. The Rockery is well worth seeing and has been described in gardening books as one of the best examples in Ireland. The pathways lead you through water features and towering trees, with rustic bridges crossing over the water garden. The walled garden is home to vegetables and herbs as well as many varieties of soft fruit.

To visit the Lisselan estate will cost €6 per adult and under 12's are free. The gardens are open from 9am to 5pm in the winter and 9am to dusk in the summer.

Blackwater Valley, Dinosaurs & Donkeys

County Cork
www.blackwater.ie/
www.dinocafe.com/
www.thedonkeysanctuary.ie/

Blackwater Valley

The Blackwater Valley in Ireland is defined by the course of the Blackwater River that winds it way along 105 miles (169 km) from Lismore in County Wexford to Millstreet in County Cork. There is something for everyone in this area, with outdoor sports being high on the list. Hiking, riding, mountain biking and canoeing are just a few of the more energetic sports. For something calmer try a spot of fishing in one of the best stocked salmon rivers in the country. There are 22 heritage sites where you step back in time and don't miss the megalithic tomb Labbacallee which has stood for 3,500 years.

There are plenty of beautiful places to stay from B&B to smart hotels, with restaurants serving locally produced food from the wonderful and fertile farmland that stretches across the valley.

Donkey Sanctuary

The Donkey Sanctuary in Liscarroll has so far taken in 2,850 donkeys from across Ireland, many of them abandoned or who suffered as work animals. The donkeys here are guaranteed loving care and individual attention with quiet voices to calm them and food and medical care. If a group of donkeys arrive together they stay in that group, or if a single donkey comes in he or she will be paired with another donkey for companionship.

There is marked pathway round the Sanctuary so visitors can wander round freely and meet the residents and there is always staff on hand to answer any questions. The Visitor Centre has a donkey related gift shop where you can find out about adopting, fostering or sponsoring a donkey. Opening hours are Monday to Friday 9am to 4.30pm and weekends and bank holidays 10am to 5pm. There is no admission charge but all donations are welcomed as the Sanctuary relies on donations to keep running.

Dinosaur Exhibition & Cafe

For somewhere different for lunch find the Dinocafé in Castletownroche and eat surrounded by some prehistoric friends. Dinocafé was created by a sculptor and model-maker and his fascination with dinosaurs led him to build an exhibition in Ireland. He created some of the models in Lost World and Walking with Dinosaurs so has had plenty of practice with these sometimes giant creatures. A small team help create the masterpieces including expert designers, artists, painters and a great technician who puts all the parts together. The Dino Café and exhibition is open every day except for some bank holidays.

Fitzgerald's Park

Mardyke Walk
Cork
Tel: +353 21 427 0679

On the banks of the River Lee the 18 acres of Fitzgerald Park stretches out like a green oasis from the city centre. The park is a tranquil place just to go for a stroll or take the children and feed the ducks and swans. There are pretty tinkling fountains and other water features to see as well as busts and statues. Make sure you go for a walk across Shakey Bridge as it spans the river. The official name is Daly's Bridge after the local business man who contributed towards the cost of building it and it is the only suspension bridge in Cork city. The 160 foot (48 metre) long span does wobble and shake if you run across it, hence the locals name of Shakey Bridge. The park is open from 11am to 4pm but closes from 1pm to 2.15pm for lunch.

Cork Public Museum

Fitzgeralds Park, The Mardyke, Cork.
Tel: + 353 21 427 0679
www.corkcity.ie/

There are some striking archaeological finds in the Cork Public Museum including Irelands oldest pick and shovel which was found by Bronze Age miners digging for copper.

There are also Iron Age Cork Helmet Horns that show off the craftsmanship of early medieval times. Some of the collections come from as far away as the South Sea Islands, New Zealand and Australia. There are magnificent displays of Cork silver with its special hallmark and beautiful Yougal Lace. The origins of Cork are easy to see from the many objects that have been discovered in and around the town.

Originally the home of the Beamish family for decades, the museum is in a Georgian house which used to be called The Shrubberies. The museum was opened in 1910 and extended in later years with the Riverside café being included as part of the plans. The Cork Museum is open from 11am to 4pm Monday to Friday but closes from 1pm to 2.15pm for lunch. The same hours apply on Saturday but the museum closes at 4pm and on Sundays from April to September the times are 3pm to 5pm. Admission is free.

Lewis Glucksman Art Gallery

University College Cork
College Road
Cork
Tel: +353 21 490 1844
www.glucksman.org

The Lewis Gluckman Gallery is in the grounds of the University College of Cork and has display spaces, a gallery shop and lecture facilities.

The award-winning gallery building promotes the research, exploration and creation of the visual arts as well as being a educational and cultural centre.

There is an al fresco bistro for light meals and refreshments. Admission to the gallery is free but a donation of €5 is suggested towards the upkeep. The gallery is closed on Monday but open 10am to 5pm on Tuesday, Wednesday, Friday, Saturday and Sunday.

Recommendations for the Budget Traveller

Places to Stay

Paddy's Palace

Kinlay House Cork
Bob & Joan's Walk
Shandon
Cork
Tel: +353 21 450 8966
www.paddyspalace.com/

Only a few minutes' walk to the heart of the city centre with its bars, shops and restaurants is Paddy's Palace. It has a 24 hour reception and you can come and go as you please and eat a free breakfast. There is a TV lounge, internet access, laundry and luggage services as well as a fully equipped kitchen if you fancy some home-cooked grub. There are a variety of room sizes to choose from, some with private bathrooms but not in all rooms. A bed in a dormitory is from just €15 while for €18/person you can book a private room.

Bru Bar Hostel

57 MacCurtain Street
Cork
Tel: +353 21 455 9667
www.bruhostel.com/

The owners of the Bru Bar have plenty of experience in hospitality and micro-brewing and have put this to good use in creating a lively hostel for a stay in Cork. The hostel is close to the train and bus stations and near to the heart of the city for you to enjoy the best night out. The hostel has live music most nights and offers some great quality and unusual beers.

There are dormitory style rooms and private rooms for accommodation and the prices start from €15 per night. All the rooms have private facilities but they are not all en-suite. There is a basic breakfast included but bacon rolls are on sale downstairs every morning. Weekly rates can reduce the price slightly and for backpackers from Australia and New Zealand there is a discount for travelling so far!

Stanley Guest House

Stanley House, Colla Road, Schull, West Cork
Tel: +353 28 28425
www.stanley-house.net/

For great views and a good night's sleep Stanley House in the village of Schull is just right.

With stunning views from all the centrally heated bedrooms as well as the sun room across Schull Harbour it is certainly a relaxing place. The rooms are comfortable and spotlessly clean and the varied breakfast menu features home-baked goodies and free range eggs. The bedrooms are all en-suite and have a hospitality tray, hairdryer, TV, electric blankets, toiletries and Wifi. All this homely luxury will cost from €38 per person per night and that includes a super breakfast.

Mountain View B&B

Meens
Newmarket
County Cork
Tel: +353 872741809
www.enjoy-our-hospitality.com/

Mountain View B&B offers comfortable accommodation which is about an hour's drive from many of the county's most famous attractions. There are just two rooms and up to five people can be accommodated. Both the bedrooms are en-suite with hospitality trays, hairdryer and free Wifi. A full Irish breakfast is offered and vegetarian, vegan and gluten free diets can be catered for, but let them know in advance.

Rates are €27.50 per person per night in a shared room and discounts are offered for longer stays. Dogs are welcome to stay as long as they are house-trained. The B&B is in an ideal location for competitors on the Munster dog show circuit.

Annabella Lodge

Mallow
County Cork
Tel: +353 022 43 991
www.annabellalodge.com/

Annabella Lodge is a few minutes outside of Mallow town centre where there are restaurants and bars to sample the locally produced foods. The train station is close by with regular services to Dublin, Cobh, Cork, Midleton and the Kerry area. On your arrival you will be welcomed with home baked goods and a cup of tea or coffee. There is dry storage for golf clothing, equipment and shoes and they can supply information on local golf courses and events.

The six bedrooms are all en-suite with hospitality tray, toiletries and electric blankets on request. The guest lounge has free email so you can keep in touch with friends and family and there is free Wifi all across the property. A super Irish breakfast is served in the sunny conservatory every day. Guests can help themselves to cereals, fruit juice and hot drinks while waiting for their choice of hot breakfast to be freshly cooked. Expect to pay €30-€40 per person per night sharing a double room and €35-€45 for single room. The rate includes breakfast.

Places to Eat & Drink

Farmgate Restaurant & Country Store

Coolbawn,
Midleton
County Cork
Tel: + 353 21 463 2771
www.farmgate.ie/

The food at Farmgate Café all comes from local producers, cheese is made by the local dairy, fish is caught from the Ballycotton Pier and the meat is all locally reared. The food style is simple but with a mixture of traditional and Irish flair thrown in.

The prices on the lunch menu start from €4.50 and there are lunchtime specials available as well as a takeaway menu. The dinner menu ranges between €5 and €30. The restaurant is open Tuesday to Saturday for lunch from 9am to 5pm and for dinner 6.30 to 9.30. Closed on Monday.

Cobh Heritage Centre Restaurant

Cobh Heritage Centre, Cobh, County Cork,
Tel: +353 21 481 3591
www.cobhheritage.com/

The restored Victorian Railway Station and Heritage centre are well worth visiting for the history alone but if you are hungry the restaurant here is very popular. Lunches, sandwiches and pastries are served all day, all made from locally grown or produced ingredients. Open seven days a week, Monday to Saturday 9.30 to 5.15pm and Sundays and bank holidays 11am to 5.15pm. Lunches cost between €4-€7.

The Cobb Heritage Centre tells the story of the 6 million children and adults who emigrated from Ireland between 1848 and 1950. Cobh was the departure point for 2.5 million who left to find a different life in a foreign country, making it the Ireland's largest point of emigration.

O'Connors Seafood Restaurant

Wolfe Tone Square, Bantry, County Cork.
Tel: +353 275 5664
www.oconnorseafood.com/

Pots of mussels and a tankful of live lobsters plus an exciting dish of monkfish and smoked venison risotto are just a few of the delicious sounding dishes on the O'Connors menu.

The menu is often changed and the daily specials are chosen from the catch of the day from the local fishermen.

The restaurant is open daily from 12 noon for lunch and dinner and there is an Early Bird evening menu from 5.30pm to 7pm every day with two courses just €20 or three courses for €25. On the á la carte menu the roast of the day is €10 with plenty of other reasonably priced dishes to choose from.

La Jolie Brise Pizza & Grill

The Square
Baltimore
County Cork
Tel: +353 28 20441
www.waterfrontbaltimore.ie/

La Jolie Brise is a family restaurant in the village of Baltimore. This pretty village with its harbour is a great place for families to come and enjoy the hospitality that Ireland offers. This restaurant opens at 8.30am for breakfast where you can have a continental style breakfast or a full Irish and then relax afterwards with a cappuccino or hot chocolate and admire the views across the harbour. The quality of the food is excellent and the prices are affordable. Meals are available all day until 11pm Friday to Sunday and 10pm Monday to Thursday.

Locals and tourists rub shoulders at La Jolie Brise and can choose from handmade Italian pizzas, Roaring Water Bay mussels, oysters, prawns and steaks all served with chips and homemade salad. Children are welcome and in the summer there is an outside seating area to make the most of the weather.

Café Paradiso

16 Lancaster Quay
Cork City
Tel +353 21 427 7939
www.cafeparadiso.ie/

This is a vegetarian restaurant but dedicated meat lovers will be pleased to know there is hardly a lentil in sight. The menu has tempting items like potato and black kale gnocchi in sage & cider butter and maple-glazed king oyster mushrooms on a leek & walnut croustade.

The menu changes with the seasons so only the freshest produce is used. This is one of the best vegetarian restaurants for miles around, not just for main meals but the desserts surpass all expectations as well.

The food is all lovingly prepared with high quality ingredients and the menu is wide and varied. There is a fixed price pre-theatre menu available until 7pm which is a good value option. Café Paradiso is open for lunch on Saturdays from 12 noon to 2.30pm and for dinner Monday to Saturday from 5.30pm to 10pm.

Places to Shop

The English Market

Grand Parade
Cork
Tel: +353 21 492 4258

There is so much to choose from in this market it is hard to know where to start. Most of the produce is local with smoked salmon, sausages, hams, cheeses and breads all piled high just waiting to tempt you.

A few imports like wine and olive oil are available just to add in to your shopping basket. If you are on a self-catering holiday or looking for picnic ingredients this will be heaven on earth. Fresh fish and shellfish abounds but if you are not sure how to prepare it the friendly fishmongers will be more than happy to help with suggestions.

The market has been here selling food to local and visitors alike for nearly 400 years and it was on the Queen's list of places to see when she visited Cork. The English Market is open six days a week from 9am to 5pm and closed Sundays.

Quills Woollen Market

Ballingeary
County Cork
Tel: +353 64 663 2277
www.irishgiftsandsweaters.com/

Quills Woollen Market is known across the world for producing high quality gifts and Irish knitwear at sensible prices.

The family run business is now in it's third generation and started in 1938. The unique cardigans and Aran sweaters that Quills is proud to sell are all hand-knitted by local ladies and while some may have the same pattern, each garment will be unique. There are beautiful styles to choose from for men, women and children in not just wool but tweed, mohair and linen.

Dunnes Stores

Tel: +353 21 483 5341
www.dunnesstores.com/

Ben Dunne was a man with a vision, he wanted to give everyone the chance to buy good quality items at decent prices, and he called it Better Value. It was in Cork in 1944 that the first Dunnes store opened and the crowds flooded through the doors in a frenzy of buying. After being starved of shopping through the war years the opportunity to buy clothes again was eagerly grasped by the people of Cork.

Move forward several decades and the Dunnes empire has 155 stores across the Republic of Ireland, Northern Ireland, Scotland, England and Spain. The Better Value promise had been kept and fashion wear, goods for the home and quality foods are available at affordable prices. There are 14 Dunnes in County Cork and opening times and locations are all on the website.

SuperValu

Tel: +353 1850 211 840
www.supervalu.ie/

The SuperValu chain of stores is part of Ireland's largest food and grocery distributor, the Musgrave Group. There are 193 stores throughout Ireland with many being in the county of Cork. The stores have been serving the people of Ireland for over 30 years with a combination of friendly service, quality and good value. The stores sell a combination of foodstuffs, furniture, clothing and small household items.

Homestore + More

Unit 10, Mahon Point Retail Park,
Mahon Link Road
Cork
Tel: + 353 21 435 9742
www.homestoreandmore.ie/

If you are looking for a selection of products at affordable prices for the home look no further.

The thirteen nationwide stores of homestore + more offer a superb range of products of unrivalled quality. The first homestore + more opened in 2004 and with their policy of value, brilliant customer service and friendly staff the company has grown into Ireland's leading store for bedroom, bathroom and kitchen items. The Cork city store is open Monday to Friday from 9am to 9pm, Saturday 9am to 7pm and Sunday & bank holidays from 11am to 6.30pm.

Galway

On the west coast of the Emerald Isle of Ireland is County Galway. In the west, Connemara has mountains (the highest is Benbaun at 729 metres), peat bogs and a rocky coastline with fjords. The Connemara National Park is beautiful and close to Kylemore Abbey. The Victorian Walled Gardens has a story to tell. Just a short ferry ride away are the Aran Islands where you can visit for some peace and quiet.

The eastern two-thirds of County Galway are a contrast to the west with a flat landscape and many rivers and small lakes. Lough Corrib is where County Galway meets County Mayo and is the largest lake in the Republic of Ireland where you can take a cruise on the smooth waters.

To the north of the county is Clifden, the main town of the Connemara region. The town became famous when Guglielmo Marconi chose to build his fixed wireless service here in 1905. It was to be the first point-to-point communication between North America and Europe and opened to the public in 1907 with a 10,000 word transmission. Marconi chose Clifden as it was the closet point to Glace Bay where the sister station was. At one point over 400 people were employed by Marconi in Clifden.

Galway City itself is crammed full of historical and cultural buildings and areas of interest, many dating back to early Christian times. They have nearly all been well preserved and the city dwellers just accept them as part of their everyday lives. Galway has produced many great artistic and literary greats and the history of these people lives on through the numerous cultural experiences offered.

Shopping in Galway City means browsing round a mixture of large or small stores, looking at handmade or man-made items, both ancient and modern. From the big brand stores to many local handicraft shops there is whole wealth of goods waiting to tempt you. Round every corner there is a new bookshop or boutique with attractive window displays hoping to entice passers-by in.

The main shopping areas are the pedestrianised streets round Quay Street then the Latin Quarter, Eyre Square and Dominick Street. In Dominick Street the Bridge Mill has been converted into a small shopping centre with gift and craft shops as well as a coffee shop, wine bar and art gallery. Kirwan's Lane is an excellent example of architecture from the 16th and 17th centuries and this mediaeval treasure is lined with craft shops and individual shops as well as several restaurants and bars. The Saturday Market between Shop Street and Market Street is a well patronised market come rain or shine. Locals and visitors rub shoulders as they jostle each other to see the wide variety of fresh fruit and vegetables, herbs and fresh baked goods on display. The sound of sausages sizzling adds to the generally buzz of the market with stall-holders and customers vying with each other to make the most noise.

Proof that Galway has been inhabited for many years came to light when evidence of shellfish middens were discovered. Oysters were a very popular food source in Roman times and the proximity of oyster beds made certain places worth developing into towns. By the twelfth century, the Normans were in control and in 1270 they built walls round the city as defences. International trading then began with ships sailing to and from the West Indies and Spain. The Spanish Arch in Galway City is a sign of the influence the Spanish had on the town.

Culture

When arriving in Galway City a good way to get a feel for the place would be to take an organised bus tour. Galway City Tours offer a hop-on hop-off system that takes in up to 25 of the best attractions and highlights of the city. http://www.galwaybustours.ie/. Through the daytime the streets will be thronged with shoppers and workers going about their business. By early afternoon the pubs start to fill up as young and old come out for a pint of the black stuff. When the pubs close the partying spills out into the streets and can carry on until early morning.

The university city of Galway has an atmosphere of culture mixed in with plenty of outdoor activities and national sports and is known as Ireland's Cultural Heart. There are plenty of social activities in the numerous bars, pubs and clubs where traditional Irish music and hospitality can found all day and night. There are festivals and events for nearly everything in County Galway, walking, marathons, cycling, mussels, fishing, football, canoe polo, a bog festival, currach racing, films, food, quilts and hurling, the list is pretty endless. If you are in Ireland in March be sure not to miss a St Patricks day event somewhere. www.stpatricksfestivalgalway.com

There are art weeks, culture weeks and also live entertainment weeks where up to 50 musicians perform in and around the city. Within the city there are approximately 50 event venues with the main ones being Spanish Parade next to the Spanish Arch and Eyre Square containing John F. Kennedy Park. In 2007 Galway came in at number eight on the world's sexiest city list.

Every September up to 10,000 people swarm into Galway for the Galway International Oyster Festival. This is one of the city's biggest festivals and fine wines, gourmet food and entertainment abound with copious quantities of oysters and Guinness of course.
www.galwayoysterfest.com

For horse-racing fans the racecourse is just a short distance from the town centre. Several race meetings are held every year with all the glitz and glamour that goes with this lifestyle. They even have their own Ladies Day and around 150,000 people attend the Summer Festival every year. www.galwayraces.com. On the subject of horses there is the Ballinasloe International October Fair & Festival which is more of a typical country show but centres around everything equine. The nine day event has a great community feeling and there is plenty to do and see. There is live music, food, arts and crafts and plenty to keep the children occupied. Join the 85,000 other people that go every year and have some fun.
www.ballinasloe.com

In July every year the Galway Arts Festival takes place with its famous Macnas parade. Macnas is a performance company based in Galway but has entertained audiences in 20 different countries across the globe. The name mean Joyful Abandonment in Irish and this is exactly what the company portray in their exuberant and colourful street performances every July. They have been credited with changing Ireland's view on public displays and at the Galway Arts Festival the streets get overcrowded as thousands flock to see the show.

Galway City has two theatres, the Druid Theatre and the Town Hall Theatre, that host a variety of events between them. They offer a full programme of theatre shows from local and visiting companies, comedy, music, readings and talks.

Location & Orientation

County Galway is in the Irish province of Connacht and is on the west coast of Ireland. After County Cork it is the largest county in Ireland and is home to a large Irish speaking population. In 2011 the population of the county was 250,541 and approximately 78% of this number are white Irish, direct descendants of the Norman settlers and native Gaelic peoples. Around 17% are non-Irish and the remainder are foreign born Irish.

To get to County Galway there is a choice of car, coach or train or flying into Knock or Shannon Airports both about 50 miles away. The airport at Carnmore in Galway City closed in 2011 as the runway was too short to accommodate large commercial aircraft. Connemara airport to the west of the region has flights to the Aran Islands and Inis Bó Finne Island.

Most Galwegians use buses to get around both in the city and throughout the county. Several different bus companies operate the routes including scheduled services to Dublin, Dublin Airport, Limerick, Cork and Clifden. The main rail and bus station is Ceannt Station at Fairgreen in the heart of the city. Ceannt Station opened in 1851 and there is a proposed major development for the area including the station and the surrounding land.

Road links are good with three primary national roads. Plans are being made to develop the Galway-Dublin, Galway-Limerick and Galway-Tuam routes into dual carriageways or maybe motorways.

By sea there are regular freight and passenger ferry services between Galway and its various islands. Galway Harbour is earmarked for major development should funds be agreed.

Climate & When to Visit

County Galway has a fairly limited range of seasonal change of temperature. The city is a major tourist destination and experiences all four seasons but without the extremes found in some places. One sure thing about the Irish weather is that rain will fall at some point in every month of the year and quite heavily in the autumn months. There is some 90mm of rainfall in October.

The summer months see an average of around 18°C to 20°C with a fair amount of rain falling. In autumn the temperature drops quite quickly to 9°C in October and 5°C by November. The daytime high can be 14-16°C but mornings and evenings will definitely have a nip in the air. If you are lucky in winter the mercury might reach 7°C but is more likely to hover around the 2°C mark. January is the coldest month but once the month is out the temperature starts to rise quite quickly. By March it can be up to 12°C and as much as 15°C in April.

Spring is always a pleasant time to visit when the dampness of winter is leaving and the promise of warm summer days are just round the corner. A few layers of clothing are always the best idea as the sunny days can still be chilly when the sun disappears behind the clouds. Galway as a county very rarely used to see snow, frost and hail but with climate changes over recent years the possibility of this happening seems to increase as each year passes. If you plan to visit the county in the winter months make sure you have sufficiently warm clothing and some decent, snow proof footwear.

Sightseeing Highlights

Galway Bay & Salthill Promenade

Galway Bay is about 30 miles long and between and 6 and 18 miles wide. The best way to take in the stunning scenery is to go for a drive heading out from Galway City at the top of the bay. Head west towards Spiddal passing Barna Woods on your right and on the left you can listen to the sound of the sea crashing onto the rocks below.

There are plenty of side roads leading down to the cliffs with places to park so take your time and enjoy the fresh sea air. A good place to stop is just before the Loughinch River where there are good opportunities to take spectacular photos across the bay. If you head south from Galway City towards Kinvarra the road is more or less at sea level and the stone walls hold back verdant green fields. There are numerous inlets and rivers and some amazing views across to the Aran Islands.

If a walk sounds better than a drive then take a wander along the two mile long Salthill Promenade in Galway City. Overlooking Galway Bay the promenade is great for walking, jogging, cycling or rollerblading. There are benches along the way so take time to sit down and admire the views all the way across the County Clare. If you fancy a dip in the sea the Blackrock diving platform is still there. The platform is a left-over from when the area was a popular bathing spot in the 1950's and it is still used by a few brave souls to get into the sea rather than the safer method of the nearby steps.

Turoe Pet Farm & Leisure Park

Bullaun,
Loughrea,
County Galway,
Tel: +353 091 841 580
http://www.turoepetfarm.com

Turoe Farm opened in 1993 and is now one of the best visitor attractions in the west of Ireland.

The farm is family run and offers great value for money with excellent customer service. There is always something going on around the 14 acre park no matter what the weather conditions. Walk round the park and have a cuddle with the animals or have a go at feeding the young ones. There are friendly llamas and alpacas who will happily pose for photos as well as goats, sheep, donkeys and ponies. The pond is full of ducks and geese and don't forget to pay a visit to The Wishing Well.

If the weather is wet there is always Inflatable City, one of Europe's largest indoor bouncing castles, to keep the children amused. The Coffee Shop serves hot drinks and snacks and sells souvenirs while the Country Kitchen has a more extensive menu if you are feeling hungry. The opening times vary widely through the year but for summer time it is generally the end of May until the end of August from 10am to 7pm. For special times like Halloween and Christmas it is worth checking on their website. The admission fee is €12 for children and €6 for adults with family passes available.

Inis Bó Finne (Island of the White Cow)

County Galway,
Tel: +353 95 45 895
www.inishbofin.com

Inis Bó Finne or Island of the White Cow lies around seven miles off the coast of Galway.

Approximately 200 people live on the island at the present time and tourism is one of the main incomes on the island along with fishing and farming. Evidence shows that Inis Bó Finne has been inhabited since 8000-4000 BC and at one time the island was used a prison for Catholic priest. The island has its own Ceili band and often plays host to visiting artists and musicians.

Visitors can take mountain walks, go hill climbing, try shore angling or dive into the clear waters surrounding the island. The beaches have won awards for safety and the pristine sands are littered with shells waiting to be collected. A rather odd aspect of the island is that there are no trees at all. Over the years any wood was cut down for fuel and as the sea air is laden with salt the trees never managed to grow again

To get to Inis Bó Finne the ferry departs from Cleggan in the Connemara region and there are three crossings a day in summer and two in winter. A bus runs straight from Galway City to Cleggan each day. For staying on the island there are a range of hotels, B&B's, hostels and a few camping places as well as private house and apartment rentals. Most of the bigger hotels have restaurants and there are various other bars and places to eat. The community centre has a playgroup and sells a selection of books and items relating to the island.

Leisureland Galway

Salthill Promenade
Galway City
Tel: +353 91 521 455
www.leisureland.ie/

Leisureland is a multi-purpose leisure space in Galway with three swimming pools, a 1000 seat venue and a high tech gym. The leisure centre has won numerous awards for customer service, safety and hygiene as well as services for the disabled. The swimming area has great facilities for everyone, a 25 metre pool for serious swimmers is alongside a pirate ship and paddle boats for the little ones. A 65 metre slide and giant inflatables add to the fun for all to enjoy. The gym has all the equipment for a good work out and there are many different fitness classes. Opening times and prices do vary so it is best to check online or call in advance.

Connemara National Park

Letterfrack, County Galway
Tel: +353 95 41 054
www.connemaranationalpark.ie/

Connemara National Park opened in 1980 and the 2,957 hectares is home to some of the famous mountains of Beanna Beola or Twelve Bens range.

The whole area is rich in wildlife and there are miles of grasslands, woodlands, heaths and bogs to explore under the watchful eyes of Muckanaght, Benbrack, Benbaun and Bencullagh (a few of the Twelve Bens). The parklands were once owned by several private individuals as well as Kylemore Abbey Estate, the Letterfrack Industrial School and Richard Martin. Richard Martin, aka Humanity Dick, helped start the RSPCA in the 19th century. The Connemara National Park is now owned by the state and is solely for park purposes. Admission to the park is free and the grounds are open all year round. The Visitor Centre is open from March to October from 9am to 5.30pm daily.

Tropical Butterfly Centre

Carraroe
Connemara
County Galway

A couple of miles from Rossveale Harbour is the unique experience of the Tropical Butterfly Centre where the brightly coloured exotic butterflies fly free in a giant enclosed tropical garden. There are some very rare plants creating an atmosphere of lush splendour in this simulated natural environment. There is a small coffee shop with butterfly themed gifts and local crafts to purchase. The centre is open from May to September.

Aran Islands

http://www.aranislands.ie

The Aran Islands are a few miles off the County Clare coast at the entrance to Galway Bay. There are three islands, the smallest to the east is Inisheer, the middle one by location and size is Inishmaan and the largest one to the west is Inishmore or Aranmore. All the islanders speak Irish and the local language is used on many of the islands signs. Transport to the islands is by ferry or air and it is recommended to stay a few days to reap the benefits of the fresh air, culture and heritage. There are about 437 varieties of wild flowers across the islands and what better way to see them than by hiring a pushbike or take a tour in a pony and trap.

Coole Park National Nature Reserve

Coole Visitor Centre
Gort,
County Galway
Tel: +353 91 631 804
www.coolepark.ie/

Coole Park with Garryland covers an area of 405 hectares with about four mile of nature trails wandering through woods, limestone, furloughs and going past rivers and Coole Lake.

The Family Trail is an easy walk of a mile or so, going past the deer park, the site of the old house and ending at the Autograph Tree in the walled garden. The Seven Woods trail is a bit longer and goes through the woods made famous in the poems by W.B. Yeats. There are beautiful flowers and birds to look out for and depending on the time of year you could see butterflies and bluebells, violets and squirrels, treecreepers and swans.

The house was the home of the dramatist Lady Gregory and Coole Park was at the centre of the Irish Literary revival at the beginning of the 20th century. George Bernard Shaw and William Butler Yeats were frequent visitors and with many other literary greats they carved their initials into an old beech tree. The Autograph Tree is still standing but the actual house is long gone. The Visitor Centre is part of the old stable and across the cobbled yard are the remains of the harness and coach rooms.

Coole Park is open from Easter until the end of September from 10am to 5pm and an hour later in July and August. Admission is free, there are trail guide booklets, postcards, books and maps on sale and there is a tea room for a refreshing drink when you have wandered round the grounds.

Kylemore Abbey & Victorian Walled Gardens

Kylemore, Connemara, County Galway
Tel: +353 95 41146
www.kylemoreabbeytourism.ie/

Kylemore Abbey is stunning; there is no other word for it. Set against a backdrop of a beautiful forest with the water of Pollacapul Lough moving serenely in front, the Abbey is the stuff that fairy tales are made of. There is far more to see than just the Abbey and six acres of Victorian Walled Gardens will keep even the most avid gardener happy for hours and the beautiful Gothic church with its sad story will delight visitors.

A visit to Kylemore Abbey is a great family day out and there is a restaurant and tea room serving homemade dishes, a craft shop for picking up some locally made gifts as well as guided tours of the abbey and ample photo opportunities. There is a special play trail for children designed by local students. Throughout the abbey and grounds there are 22 pieces of play equipment made from the fallen wood of the estate trees and each telling a Kylemore story.

The abbey has been home to a group of Benedictine Nuns since 1920 and it is the only such community in Ireland. Some of the abbey is open to visitors who wish to see inside and the short tour takes in some of the rooms that have been restored since a fire in 1959 damaged much of the interior. Not all of the abbey can be viewed as the nuns live in the abbey and in return take great pride in looking after parts of the Victorian Walled Garden.

Kylemore Abbey is open all the year round and adults pay €12.50, OAP's €10 and students €9. For children under ten years old admission is free. There are various family passes available and if you book online a 10% discount applies.

Battle of Aughrim Interpretative Centre

Galway-Dublin Road (N6)
Aughrim
Ballinasloe
County Galway
Tel: +353 90 967 3939

The Battle of Aughrim tool place in July, 1961 and 9,000 of the 45,000 soldiers involved lost their lives. The course of European and Irish history was changed that day when William of Orange fought James II of England.

The centre is right next to the battlefield and it is easy to relive the sights and sounds of that day through the advent of modern technology. There is a café, bookshop and craft shop to visit as well and the opening times are Tuesday to Saturday 10am to 6pm. Ticket price is €5 for adults, €4 for students and OAP's, €3 for children and a family ticket can be purchased for €12.

Galway City Museum

Galway City Museum
Spanish Parade
Galway City
Tel: 353 91 532 460
www.galwaycitymuseum.ie/

Galway City Museum aims to preserve the history of the city and provide a space where locals and visitors can come and learn about Galway past and present. There are three floors telling the story of the city from mediaeval times to the present day, including an exhibition on the Claddagh village. Two local children have created a special Kids Museum Detective sheet so if you are visiting with children make sure they use their super-sleuthing skills on the way round. The museum is closed Sunday and Monday but open 10am to 5pm Tuesday to Saturday. Admission is free.

Corrib Princess River Cruise

Woodquay
Galway City
Tel: +353 91 592 447
www.corribprincess.ie/

Take a 90 minute relaxing river cruise on the Corrib Princess and admire the natural beauty of the waterways of River Corrib and Lough Corrib. Pass by castles standing proudly on the river banks, fishermen waiting for the catch of the day and swans vying for river space with canoeists.

The Corrib Princess is well equipped and the bar has good selection of drinks and some delicious Irish coffees. There is seating inside and out, toilets on board and the skipper points out all the most interesting points as you glide gently past. An adult ticket is €15, students and OAP's €13, children €7 and a family ticket of two adults and up to three children is €35.

Galway Cathedral

University and Gaol Roads, Cathedral Square
Galway City
Tel: + 353 91 563 577
www.galwaycathedral.ie/

Galway Cathedral has the distinction of being Europe's youngest stone cathedral, as it was constructed in the 1950's when similar buildings were being made out of concrete.

The cathedral has a rather impressive variety of art with a mosaic of the crucifixion and a statue of the Virgin. The details are mainly Gothic and Romanesque with a little bit of Renaissance added in. The cathedral is open from 8am to 6pm each day and a donation is asked for rather than a fixed entrance fee.

Recommendations for the Budget Traveller

Places to Stay

Barnacles Hostel

10 Quay Street, Latin Quarter, Galway
Tel: +353 91 568 644
www.barnacles.ie/

In the heart of Galway in the Latin Quarter is Barnacles Hostel where there are often festivals and dancing happening right outside.

The hostel is close to all the major attractions like Eyre Square, The Claddagh and the Spanish Arch. Quay Street is pedestrianised and there is a buzzing café and restaurant atmosphere that can enjoyed along with a pint of Guinness or two.

The hostel has 112 beds in a mixture of private rooms and shared dorms, with female only dorms available. The room prices start from €10 per night and this includes breakfast. There is free Wifi, 24 hour reception, a self-catering kitchen and laundry facilities. The reception staffs are friendly and will give advice on the best places to visit and can even book tickets for certain attractions.

If you want to get away without paying at Barnacles Hostel for your bed for the night all you have to do is perform for your fellow guests. Singers and musicians can get free accommodation if they are entertaining enough. There are other events as well where free accommodation can be won.

Galway City Hostel

Frenchville Lane, Eyre Square, Galway
Tel: +353 91 566 959
www.galwaycityhostel.com/

There are great views of Eyre Square from the Galway City Hostel and fantastic transport links.

The hostel is opposite the main bus and train station so getting around couldn't get any easier. There are always fellow travellers to share stories with over a beer or two or maybe plan some outings together.

The hostel has comfortable and solid beds and the bathrooms are bright and clean with plenty of hot water. There is a fully equipped self-catering kitchen if you fancy cooking up your own grub and the hostel supplies free tea and coffee all day. If you want to relax there is free TV and a selection of DVD's plus board games and free internet. Guests are offered a light breakfast to get the day off to a good start and this is included in the room rates from €15. The accommodation is in eight bedded mixed dorms. There is a 24 hour reception and they can book discounted tickets for various bus tours and ferry trips.

Lakeshore House

Ballard
Clonbur
County Galway
Tel: +353 94 954 831
www.lakeshoreconnemara.com/

Just 50 metres from the shores of Lake Corrib is the aptly named Lakeshore B&B. It is a quick five minute drive from the village of Clonbur and only 15 minutes from the Connemara region with Lough Mask, Lough Nafooey and Joyce Valley.

The house sits in rock gardens, all beautifully designed, with garden chairs for relaxing and a children's play area. There is plenty of free car parking and even a jetty with boats for hire. If the weather is not quite so good there is a pleasant lounge to relax in where there is a piano to play or a guitar to strum.

All the rooms are en-suite with hair dryers and free Wifi. Choose from double, twin or family or there is a family apartment as well. The rooms cost from €35 per person per night with various offers for longer stays. Children under 12 sharing with their parents receive a 25% discount. A full Irish breakfast is served and there is a menu to choose your favourite items from.

Árd Einne Guesthouse

Inis Mór
Aran Islands
County Galway
Tel: +353 99 61126
www.ardeinnearan.com/

Árd Einne Guesthouse has its very own beach so walking along the coastline is a great way to explore, taking in the views across to the Clare and Galway coastlines in the distance. Situated on the east side of the island the village of Kilronan is only two kilometres away where you can visit the local pub and listen to traditional Irish music.

The guesthouse had been a family business for more than 30 years and the hosts will share with you all the best places to visit on the island. The island of Inishmore is the largest of the three Aran Islands and access is by boat or small plane.

There are eight en-suite rooms all with free Wifi, a hairdryer and a hospitality tray plus a stunning sea view so waking up is always a pleasure. A traditional Irish breakfast will set you up for the day and vegetarian or special diets can be catered for. Evening meals are available as well and can be prepared while you relax in the lounge with a glass of wine. Expect to pay from €60 per night for two people sharing a twin room including breakfast.

Oak Lodge Portumna

St Brendan's Road,
Portumna,
County Galway,
Tel: +353 90 974 1549
www.oaklodgeportumna.ie/

In the east of County Galway is the River Shannon and this is where you will find the Oak Lodge. Portumna is a busy town all year round and there is always something happening. The Shorelines Arts Festival is held every year in the town which will be of great interest to anyone who likes poetry, prose, sculptures and paintings. For more active types there is hurling, cycling, swimming and running.

The River Shannon and Lough Derg are all on the doorstep for fishing and there are many more fishing hotspots within a short drive. For fishermen staying at Oak Lodge there is a fridge, drying room and a free laundry service.

Oak Lodge has five rooms, all en-suite and the prices range from €25-€35 per person per night and this includes breakfast. The rooms all have TV, a hairdryer, hospitality tray and free Wifi. A self-catering option at €20 per person per night is also available and there is a kitchen for guests to use. There are double, twin, family and single rooms to choose from.

Places to Eat & Drink

Breathnachs Bar

The Square
Oughterard
County Galway
Tel: +353 091 552 818

Breathnachs Bar is a great place for good value and tasty pub grub. They also serve breakfast, not just a full Irish with plenty of home-baked bread but delicious pancakes dripping with maple syrup. The food is simple but freshly cooked and the owner is very hands-on so the bar is well run and always busy. The dinner menu is varied and the service excellent. Food is available Monday to Sunday lunchtimes 12 noon to 3pm and evenings 6pm to 9.30pm.

Pedro's Cafe & Grill

Tuam Shopping Centre
Tuam
County Galway
Tel: +353 93 52663
www.cafetuam.com/

This is a great place for breakfast, lunch or dinner. It is a good family friendly restaurant and the choice is great from traditional breakfasts to super salads and fresh grilled meats, pizza and pasta. An unusual item is the fried egg sandwich with cheese and chicken, served with coleslaw and chips. It isn't on the menu but they will cook it by special request. There is a very tempting dessert menu and freshly ground coffee to finish your meal with. The hours are limited as it is in the Tuam shopping centre, Monday to Saturday 9am to 7pm and Sunday 12 noon to 6pm

The Forge Pub & Eatery

Moycullen Village.
County Galway
Tel: +353 91 868 944
www.theforgepubmoycullen.com/

In the heart of Moycullen village is the Forge Pub and Eatery. This is a very popular spot with locals and tourists alike and can get busy but as they have entertainment it is no hardship to wait a while for your food.

The pub is warm and inviting and the staff are friendly and families are welcome. A full Irish breakfast is €8 and main courses start at €7.50 for lunches and €13.50 for dinner. The Forge Pub and Eatery is open for breakfast Monday to Saturday 9.30am -12 noon and then from lunchtime through to dinner from 12 noon to 9pm every day.

The Bard's Den

Letterfrack,
Connemara
County Galway
Tel: +353 954 1042
www.bardsden.com

The Bard's Den is well known for not just the food they serve but as a place to go for socialising and seisúns. A seisún is maybe what the English call a jamming session where the local musicians go to make music and have a good time. In winter the fires are roaring and anytime of the year the pub's beautiful collie dog will always be pleased to see you.

Beautiful local produce, Connemara lamb, fresh seafood and Irish beef are all turned into the most wonderful home cooked traditional pub meals. The all-day menu is from €3.50 for a starter and €12.75 for a main course with a variety of daily specials. There is a good range of drinks and wines are reasonable prices to accompany the meal.

Cupán Tae

8 Quay Lane
Galway
Tel: +353 189 5000
www.cupantae.eu/

Cupán Tae is one of the stalwarts of Galway dining experiences. Everything is top class, the sweets, cakes and pastries are to die for and the service and atmosphere are perfect. There is a fantastic selection of loose leaf teas, 30 in total, and on top of all that everything is reasonably priced. One of the specials is "Eggs Benny" so make sure you try it. For those with a savoury tooth there is a selection of salads, jacket potatoes and other non-sugary goodies to sample. Cupán Tae is open Monday to Thursday 10am to 5pm, Friday and Saturday 10am to 6pm and Sunday 11am to 6pm.

Places to Shop

Penneys

Eyre Square Shopping Centre, Galway
Tel: +353 91 566 889
www.primark.ie

Cheap and cheerful and sometimes untidy is the best way to describe Penneys.

The company has 257 stores across Europe and employs 45,000 people. Penneys will be best known to many people as Primark. Everything in a Penneys store is good value, sort of like a year round sale. The styles are always up to the minute and it is very hard to visit any branch and come out without buying something. There are clothes for all the family as well as items for the home. The Eyre Square branch is open Monday to Wednesday 9am to 7pm, Thursday and Friday 9am to 9pm, Saturday 9am to 7pm and Sunday 11am to 7pm.

Fallers Sweater Shop

25 High Street
Galway City
Tel: +353 91 564 833

Fallers Sweater Shop is a brilliant place to go for some genuine good quality touristy gifts. There is a wide selection of jumpers and knitted items for all the family and even if you don't really mean to buy anything, you probably will. There is plenty of cute Guinness memorabilia as well as cups, mugs, postcards and many other souvenirs.

Royal Tara

Connolly Ave, Mervue, Galway
Tel: +353 91 705 602
www.royal-tara.com/

If you love china this is definitely the place to visit.

There are some beautiful gift ideas, for yourself as well as friends. Choose from Celtic crafts and bone china plates and cups, carved wooden trinket boxes and ceramic or glass trinkets. The staff are friendly and very helpful and there is a shipping service if you are far away from home and need your purchases sent on.

Ceardlann-Spiddal Craft & Design Studios

15 Km/11 Miles west of Galway city
www.ceardlann.com/

Ceardlann is a craft village a short drive from Galway city centre and is home to 10 different craft workers who design, create and sell their own work. There are paper crafts, ceramics, coins, basket weaving, beautiful hand woven tapestries and shawls, jewellery and lamps made from glass and a range of paintings using acrylics. The Builín Blasta Café serves a delicious selection of sweet and savoury snacks and meals and a very tempting range of hand-made chocolates.

Thomas Dillon Claddagh Gold

1 Quay Street
Galway
Tel: +353 91 566 365
www.claddaghring.ie

This is the original home of the Claddagh ring and at the back of the shop there is a tiny museum which tells the history of this legendary piece of Irish jewellery. Take care if you have a rucksack though as it can knock things over. The Thomas Dillon shop has been in existence since 1750 and is the only maker of the Original Claddagh ring with the official Irish Assay mark stamped on each ring.

The Claddagh ring or Love and Friendship ring has a long history behind it dating back to the 16th century and this is all explained in the museum. Most people nowadays don't know the whole history and the ring is generally given as a token of love and affection. How the ring is worn can tell a great deal about a person. If the heart is towards the fingernails the wearer is unattached, but if the crown is pointing upwards the fingernails the wearer is in love or married.

The shop has a great range of rings to suit all ages and budgets and if the size isn't quite correct it can be resized while you wait. There are bracelets, lockets and earrings to choose from as well as brooches and cufflinks.

Made in the USA
San Bernardino, CA
30 November 2014